Famous & Fun Favorites
13 Appealing Piano Arrangements
Carol Matz

Nothing is more motivating for students than playing something familiar. *Famous & Fun Favorites, Book 1,* is a collection of 13 carefully selected familiar songs that young students are sure to know and love. All these arrangements are playable within the first few months of piano instruction, and can be used as a supplement to any method. No eighth notes or dotted-quarter rhythms are used, and each arrangement uses only notes in the Middle C or C five-finger pattern. The optional duet parts for teacher or parent add to the fun of playing the songs. Enjoy your musical experience with these time-tested favorites!

Carol Matz

Dedicated to my niece, Micah

Second Edition
Copyright © MMIII by Alfred Publishing Co., Inc.
All rights reserved.   Printed in USA.
ISBN 0-7390-3227-5

D1307478

Alfred

Twinkle, Twinkle, Little Star

Traditional
Arr. by Carol Matz

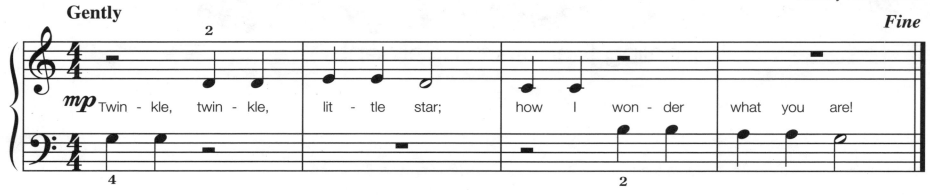

Twin - kle, twin - kle, lit - tle star; how I won - der what you are!

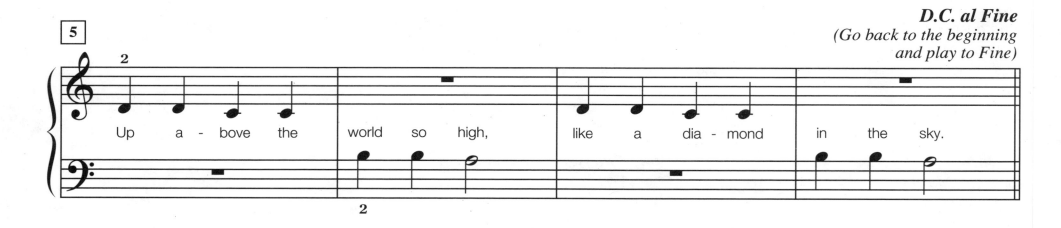

D.C. al Fine
(*Go back to the beginning and play to Fine*)

Up a - bove the world so high, like a dia - mond in the sky.

DUET PART (Student plays one octave higher)

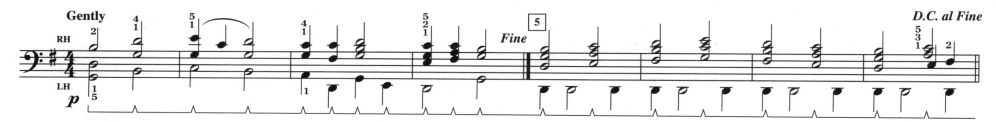

Yankee Doodle

Traditional
Arr. by Carol Matz

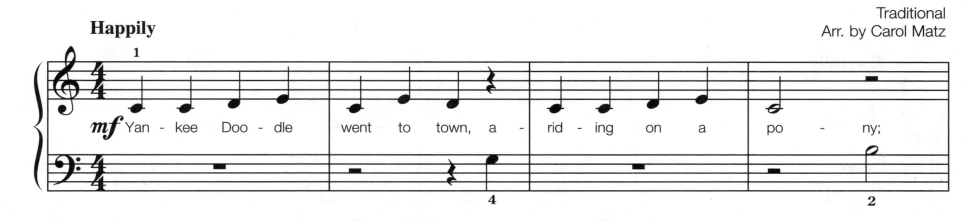

Yan - kee Doo - dle went to town, a - rid - ing on a po - ny;

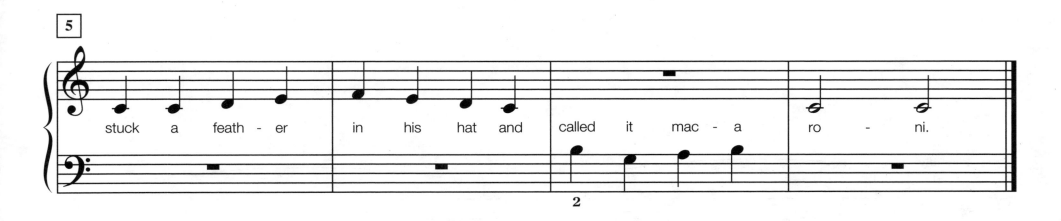

stuck a feath - er in his hat and called it mac - a ro - ni.

DUET PART (Student plays one octave higher)

Humpty Dumpty

Traditional
Arr. by Carol Matz

DUET PART (Student plays one octave higher)

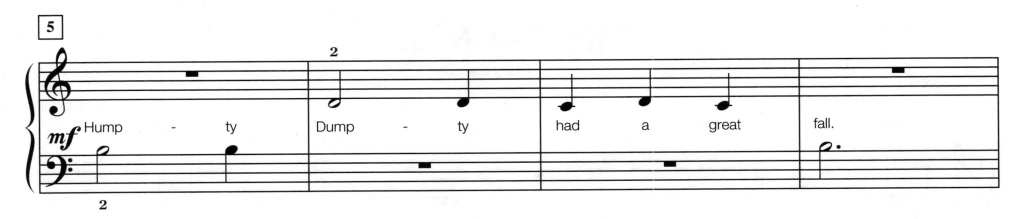

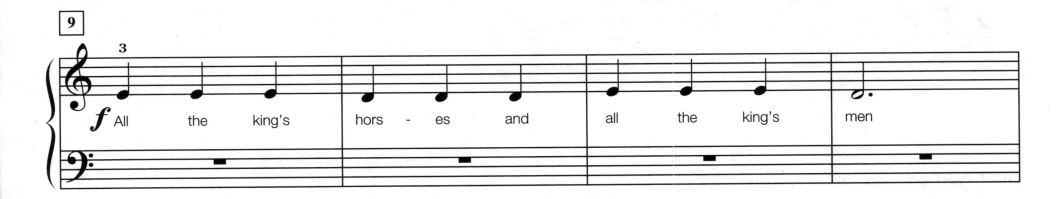

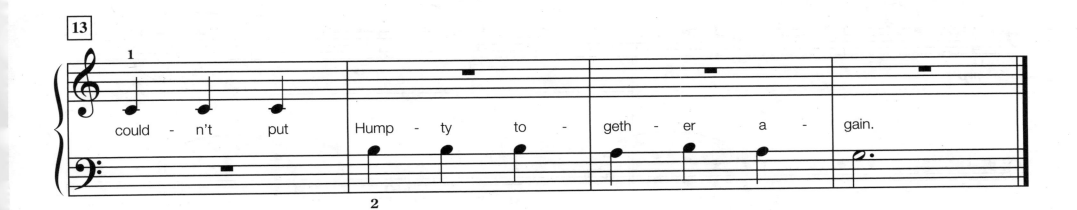

This Old Man

Traditional
Arr. by Carol Matz

Quickly

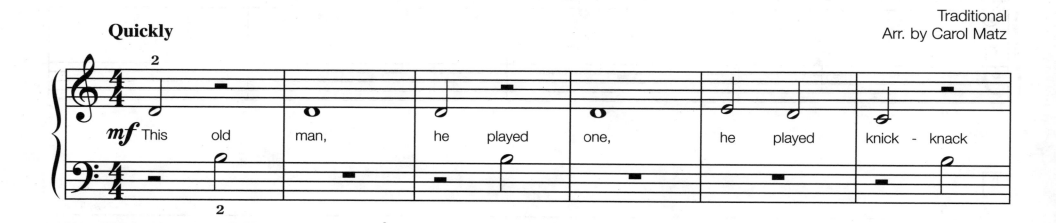

This old man, he played one, he played knick - knack

DUET PART (Student plays one octave higher)

Quickly (in two)

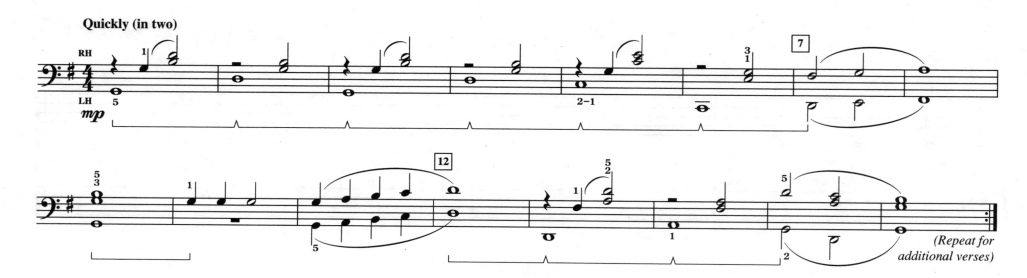

(Repeat for additional verses)

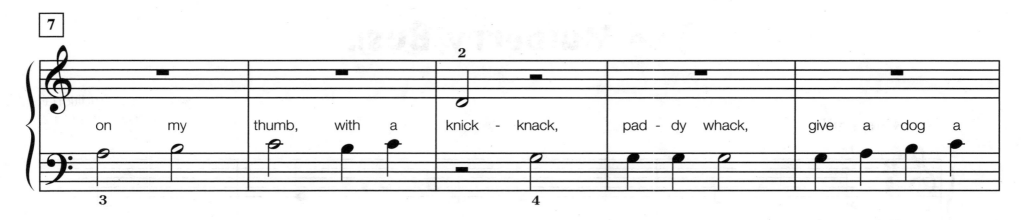

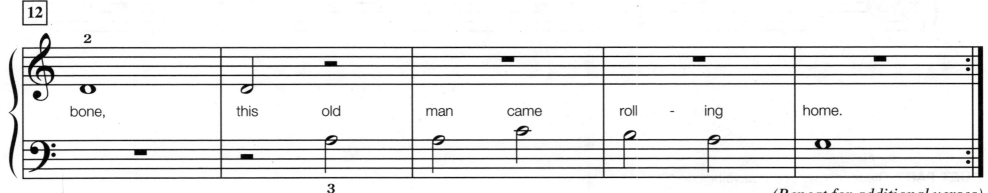

(Repeat for additional verses)

2. This old man, he played two,
   he played knick-knack on my shoe....

3. ... three ... on my knee....

4. ... four ... on my door....

5. ... five ... on my hive....

6. ... six ... on my sticks....

7. ... seven ... up to heaven....

8. ... eight ... on my gate....

9. ... nine ... on my vine....

10. ... ten ... once again....

The Mulberry Bush

Traditional
Arr. by Carol Matz

Cheerfully

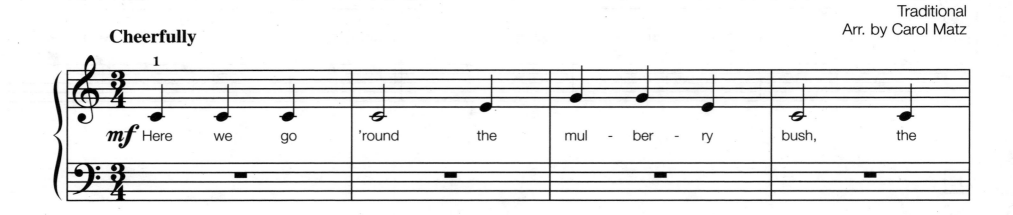

mf Here   we   go   'round   the   mul – ber – ry   bush,   the

DUET PART (Student plays one octave higher)

Cheerfully

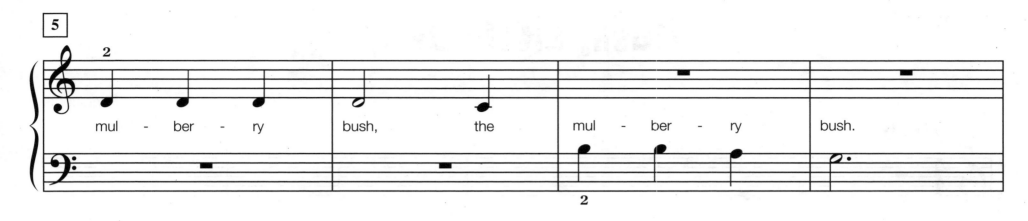

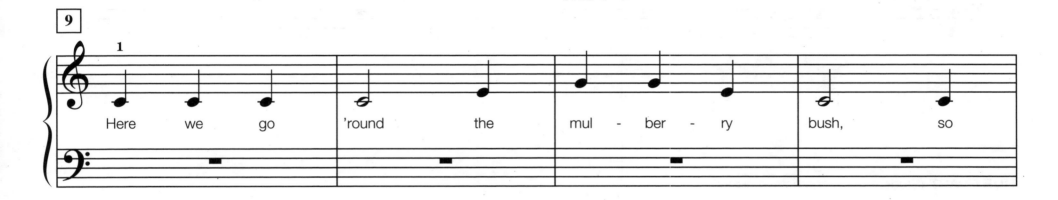

Hush, Little Baby

Traditional
Arr. by Carol Matz

Hush, lit - tle ba - by, don't say a word,

DUET PART (Student plays one octave higher)

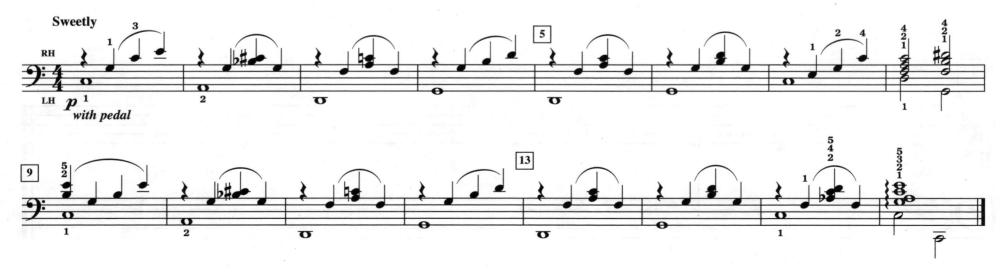

with pedal

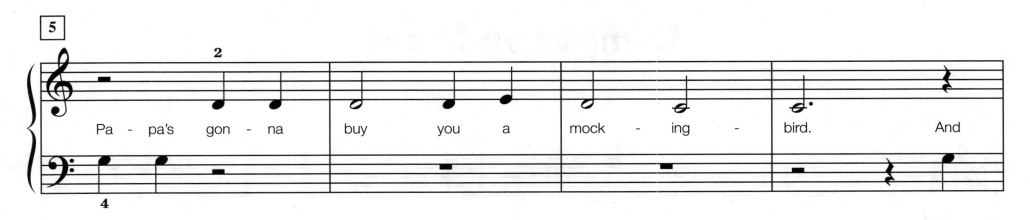

Camptown Races

Stephen C. Foster
Arr. by Carol Matz

Merrily

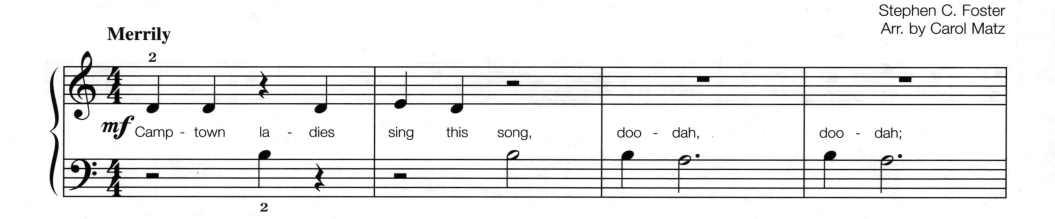

Camp - town la - dies   sing this song,   doo - dah,   doo - dah;

DUET PART (Student plays one octave higher)

Merrily

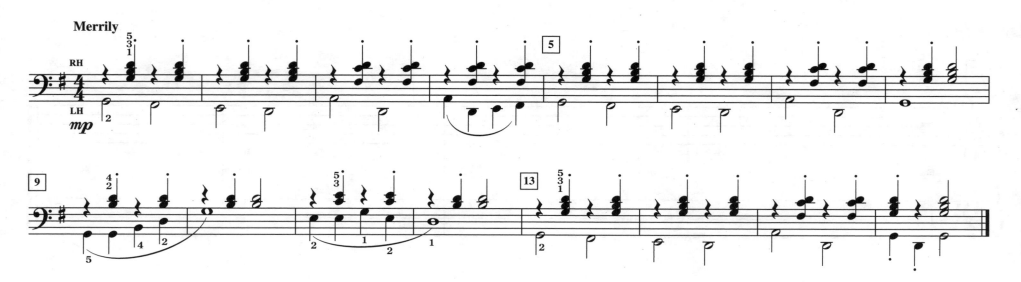

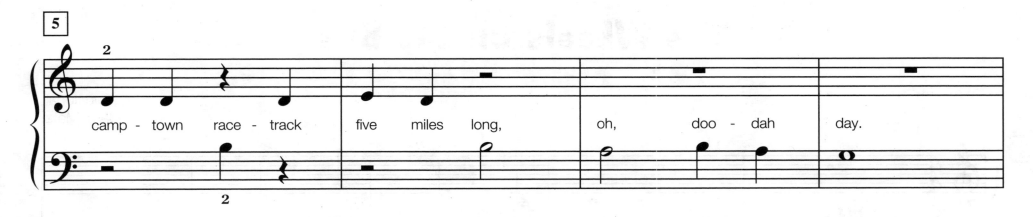

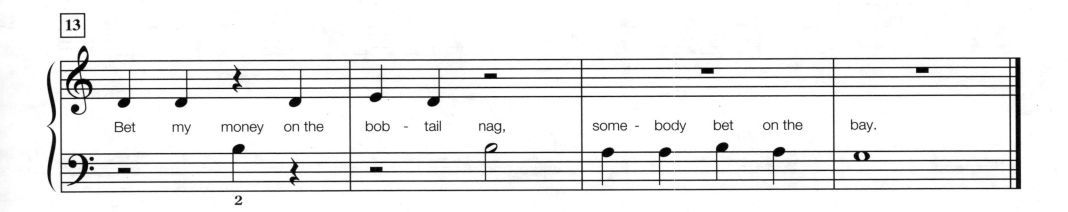

The Wheels on the Bus

Traditional
Arr. by Carol Matz

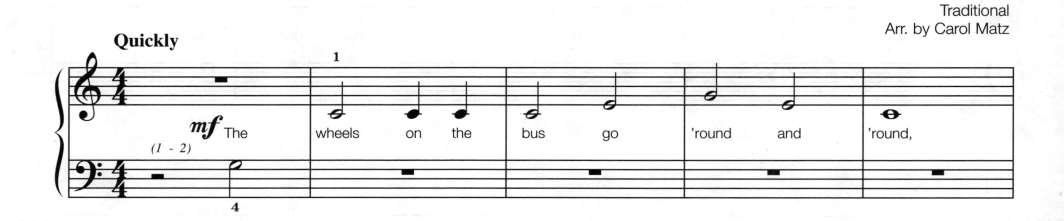

The wheels on the bus go 'round and 'round,

DUET PART (Student plays one octave higher)

(Repeat for additional verses)

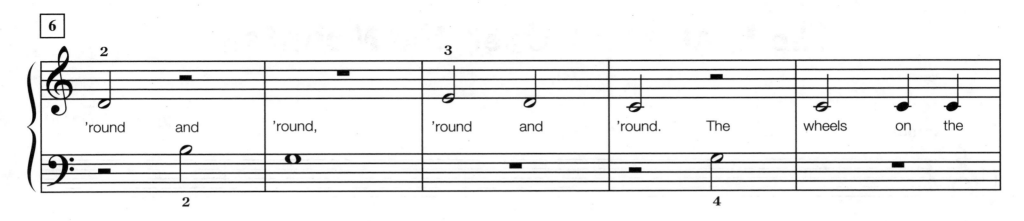

(Repeat for additional verses)

2. The wipers on the bus go "swish, swish, swish,".....

3. The people on the bus go up and down,.....

4. The horn on the bus goes "beep, beep, beep,".....

The Bear Went Over the Mountain

Traditional
Arr. by Carol Matz

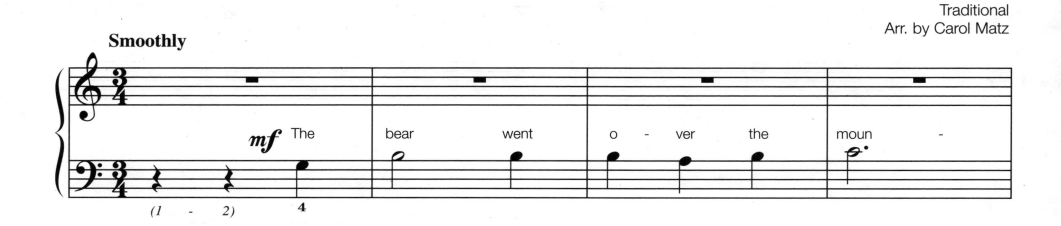

DUET PART (Student plays one octave higher)

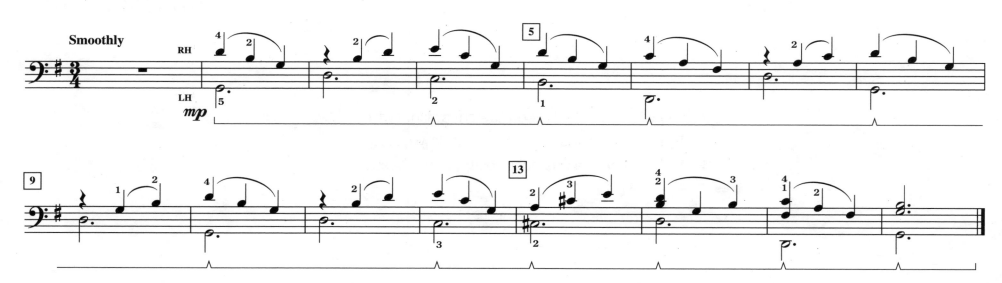

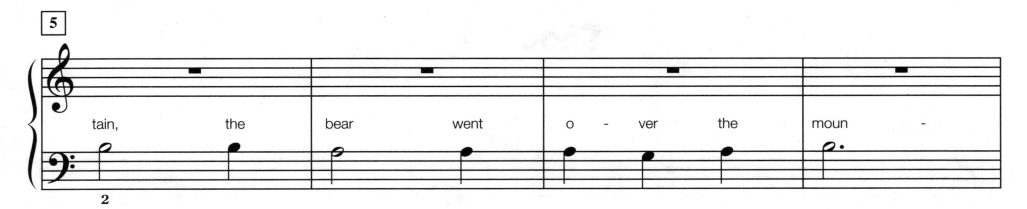

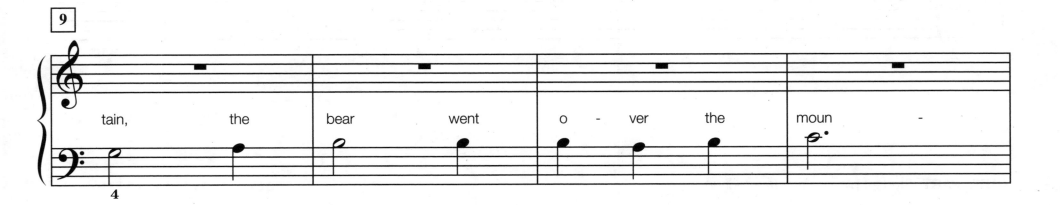

Shoo, Fly

Traditional
Arr. by Carol Matz

Brightly

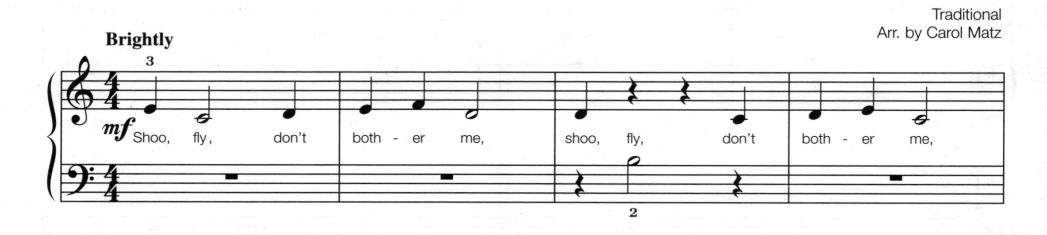

Shoo, fly, don't both - er me, shoo, fly, don't both - er me,

DUET PART (Student plays one octave higher)

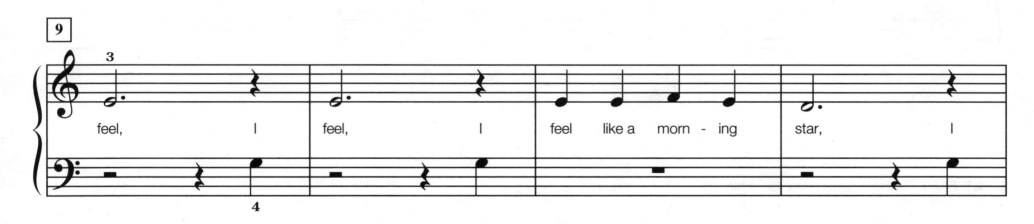

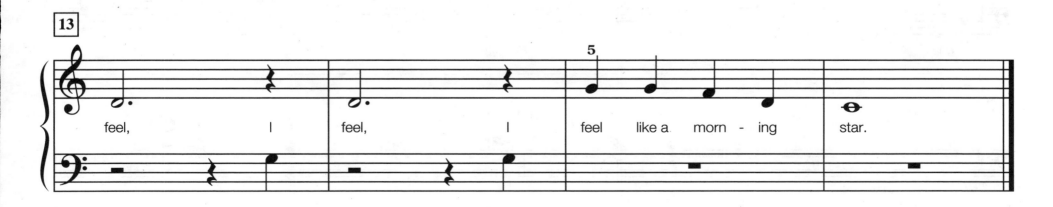

Row, Row, Row Your Boat

Traditional
Arr. by Carol Matz

Flowing

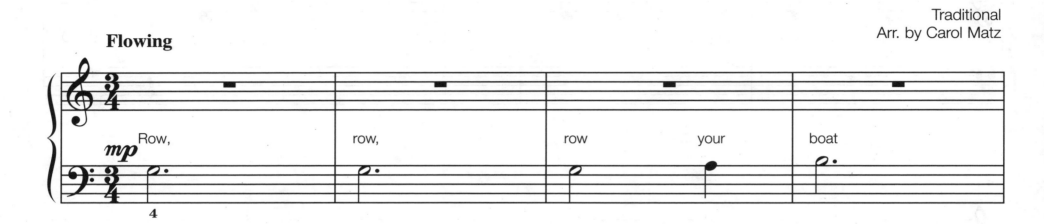

DUET PART (Student plays one octave higher)

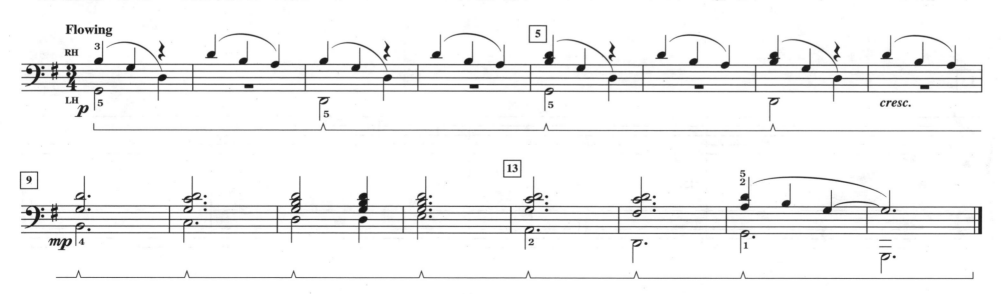

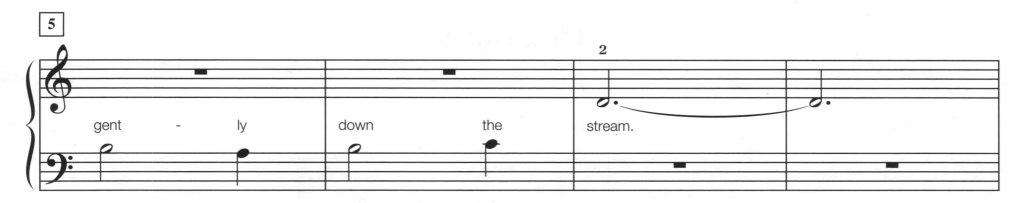

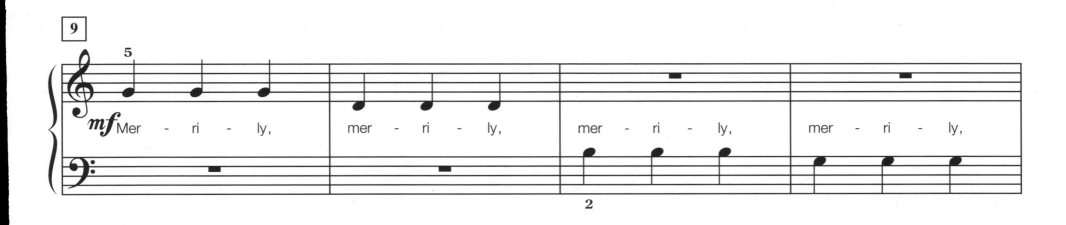

Alouette

Traditional
Arr. by Carol Matz

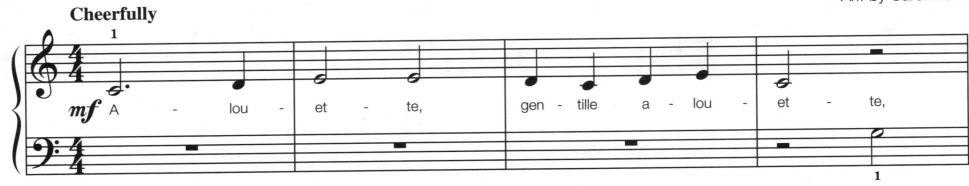

DUET PART (Student plays one octave higher)

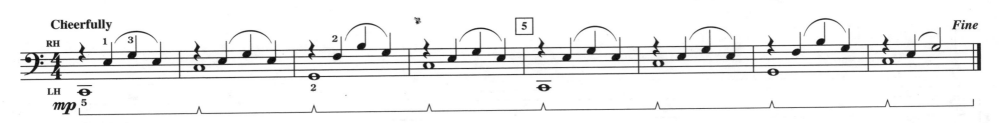

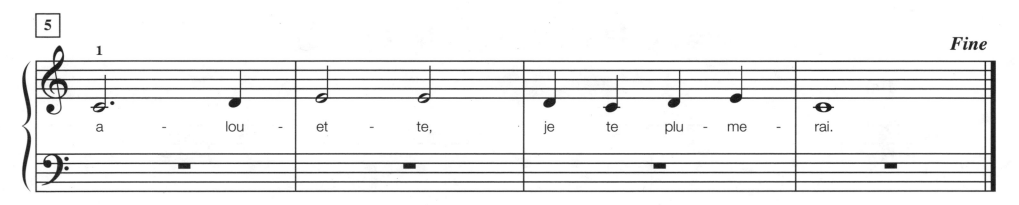

5 **Fine**

a - lou - et - te, je te plu - me - rai.

9

f Je te plu - me - rai la tête, je te plu - me - rai la tête,

D.C. al Fine
(Go back to the beginning
and play to Fine)

13

et la tête, et la tête, oh!

Mary Had a Little Lamb

Traditional
Arr. by Carol Matz

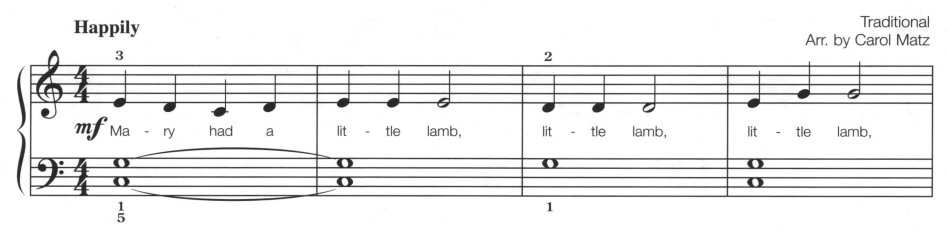

DUET PART (Student plays one octave higher)

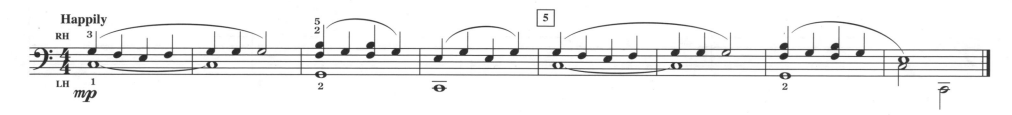

Famous & Fun Series

Christmas • Classics • Favorites • Pop • Pop Duets

Famous & Fun Favorites from the **Famous & Fun series** provides valuable supplementary material that has been carefully selected for student appeal. These effective and enjoyable arrangements can supplement any piano method and provide motivating recital material.

Highlights of the Famous & Fun series:
- carefully selected pieces
- well-graded arrangements
- levels remain consistent throughout the series
- musical, motivating arrangements
- optional duet parts (Books 1–3)

Famous & Fun Favorites, Book 1
(21392)
(Early Elementary)

Alouette
The Bear Went Over the Mountain
Camptown Races
Humpty Dumpty
Hush, Little Baby
Mary Had a Little Lamb
The Mulberry Bush
Row, Row, Row Your Boat
Shoo, Fly
This Old Man
Twinkle, Twinkle, Little Star
The Wheels on the Bus
Yankee Doodle

Famous & Fun Favorites, Book 2
(21393)
(Early Elementary to Elementary)

America the Beautiful
The Ants Go Marching
Auld Lang Syne
Bingo
Boom, Boom! (Ain't It Great to Be Crazy?)
Hickory, Dickory, Dock
John Jacob Jingleheimer Schmidt
La Cucaracha
Looby Loo
The Man on the Flying Trapeze
The Old Gray Mare
Over the River and Through the Woods
Pop! Goes the Weasel
Six Little Ducks
Take Me Out to the Ball Game
When the Saints Go Marching In

Famous & Fun Favorites, Book 3
(21394)
(Elementary to Late Elementary)

Baby Bumblebee
Down by the Bay
Home on the Range
I've Been Workin' on the Railroad
The Mexican Clapping Song
Michael Finnegan
The Noble Duke of York
Oh, My Darling Clementine
Polly Wolly Doodle
Skip to My Lou
The Stars and Stripes Forever
The Yellow Rose of Texas
You're a Grand Old Flag

Famous & Fun Favorites, Book 4
(23250)
(Early Intermediate)

America the Beautiful
Battle Hymn of the Republic
The Entertainer
The Erie Canal
Funiculi, Funicula
Greensleeves
Irish Washerwoman
La Bamba
The Riddle Song (I Gave My Love a Cherry)
The Skaters Waltz
The Snake Charmer
Swing Low, Sweet Chariot
The Thunderer
Turkey in the Straw
Wedding Tarantella
You're a Grand Old Flag

Famous & Fun Favorites, Book 5
(23251)
(Intermediate)

Alexander's Ragtime Band
America (My Country, 'Tis of Thee)
The Caissons Go Rolling Along
Carnival of Venice
Down by the Riverside
Hava Nagila
Maple Leaf Rag
Mexican Hat Dance
Sailing, Sailing
Scarborough Fair
The Star-Spangled Banner
Washington Post March
Yankee Doodle Dandy

Carol Matz is an active composer, arranger, author and editor of educational piano materials. She also maintains a piano studio where she enjoys teaching students of all ages and abilities.

Carol studied composition, arranging and orchestration at the University of Miami, with an emphasis on studio and jazz writing. In addition to her compositions and arrangements for piano, Carol has written for a variety of ensembles including orchestra, jazz big band and string quartet. Her work also includes studio arrangements and recording sessions for a number of artists in Miami-area recording studios. Carol serves as a keyboard editor for Alfred.

alfred.com

21392 Book   US $7.99

0 38081 20733 9

ISBN-10: 0-7390-3227
ISBN-13: 978-0-7390-32

9 780739 032275